Author 2 Author

A Comprehensive Guide for
Self-Published Authors

TANISHA STEWART

Author 2 Author: A Comprehensive Guide for Self-Published Authors
Copyright © 2022 Tanisha Stewart

All rights reserved.

Author 2 Author: A Comprehensive Guide for Self-Published Authors, by Tanisha Stewart. No part of this book may be reproduced in any written, electronic, recording, or photocopying form without written permission of the author, Tanisha Stewart.

Books may be purchased in quantity and/or special sales by contacting the publisher, Tanisha Stewart, by email at tanishastewart.author@gmail.com.

Editing: Cyn Anne
https://cynfulmonarch.com/collections/editing

First Edition

Published in the United States
by Tanisha Stewart

Table of Contents

Why I Wrote This Book 1

My Journey As A Self-Published Author 5

How to Use This Book 7

Manuscript Preparation 9

  Author Assistance 11

    Writing Coaches 12

    Ghostwriters 13

  Writing 15

    Character Development 16

    Plot Development 19

    Perspectives 21

    Outlining 23

  Editing 27

    Developmental Editing 29

    Self-Editing 30

    Copy/Line Editing 31

    Proofreading 32

    A Final Note 33

  Formatting 35

    eBooks 37

    Paperbacks and Hardcovers 37

- Simple Formatting versus Advanced Formatting 38
- Cover Design 41
  - Cover Elements 42
  - Choosing a Cover Designer 43
- Making it "Official" 45
  - Registering a Copyright 45
  - Obtaining an ISBN and Barcode 46
  - Pursuing an LLC 47
- Manuscript Publishing 51
  - Platforms 53
    - Kindle Unlimited 54
      - Pros of Publishing via KU 54
      - Cons of Publishing via KU 55
      - Doing Both? 56
    - Expanded Distribution 57
    - Audible 58
    - Kindle Vella 60
      - Pros of Kindle Vella 60
      - Cons of Kindle Vella 61
- Manuscript Marketing 63
  - Building a Team 65
    - Alpha Readers 65

- Beta Readers 66
- Review Teams 66
- Review Sites 67
- Email List 67

Marketing 69
- Social Media 69
  - Facebook 70
  - Instagram 70
  - Twitter 71
  - TikTok 71
  - Reader Groups 72
  - Blogs 72
- Book Signings 72
- Author Websites 73
- Amazon Ads 73
- Bookbub Ads 74
- Reader Magnets 74
- Paid Promoters 75
- Promotion Sites 76
- Developing a Strategy 76

Publishing 77
- Self-Publishing 77

- Vanity Publishers 78
- Indie Publishers 79
- Traditional Publishers 81

Finding Your Audience 83
- Reader Groups 84
- Email List 84
- Author Pages 85
- Top 100 Lists 85
- Reviews Top 100 Books 86
- Reviews on Your Books 86

Release Strategies 87
- Series 87
- Standalones 88

Manuscript Optimization 89
- Author's Notes and Bios 89
- Connecting Books 91
- Requesting Reviews 91

Odds and Ends 93
- Cross-Promotions 93
- Review Swaps 94
- Tagged Releases 94
- Reader Engagement 95

Author Website..95
Amazon Author Central 95
Goodreads 96
How to Publish on Kdp 97

Author 2 Author

Why I Wrote This Book

Like many new or aspiring authors, I had no idea what I was doing when I first started. When I learned a person could self-publish a book on Amazon, I felt like a little fish in the middle of an ocean. I was used to going to the library or bookstores to find books, not ordering them from Amazon, so I had no idea about what was entailed in the world of self-publishing.

From my preliminary research, I knew I needed to hire an editor and cover designer at the very least. Where was I going to find an editor? This was my first major hurdle. Not only did I have no idea where to look, I also was afraid that whoever I sent my book to might not be reputable, and in the worst case scenario, they might even steal my book. When I started writing my debut novel, I reached out to what I later learned was a vanity publishing company. I corresponded with an individual from this company for two years as I wrote the book. I was told the price would be around ten thousand dollars for the company to edit, create a cover, and publish my book. I didn't have this amount of money lying around, but I pressed on anyway, hoping that by the time the book was finished, I would find a way to come up with the funds.

When the book was halfway finished, I reached out to my correspondent at the publishing company and found out that she had left the company under mysterious circumstances. This threw me for a loop because I had tons of emails back and forth with this individual. Her departure from the company turned out to be a blessing in disguise. I looked up some reviews of the company (something I hadn't done before) and found that they had a reputation for scamming authors by charging exorbitant fees and then not paying royalties.

I was heartbroken to say the least. After this, I experienced a year of writer's block. Regardless of what I tried the story would not move forward. Finally, the words began to flow again. I searched the internet for another editor (this time taking company reviews into account) and found one. The website looked professional and the editor seemed to offer exactly the type of editing I was looking for. I reached out to her, and we began corresponding. Two years later, my book was finally finished, and I sent it to her.

During the process of developing my debut novel, I read tons of articles, emailed my editor incessantly, and felt like I had a handle on things. Yet, I felt that I had no idea what I was doing simultaneously. My editor kept telling me to give it time and some things could only be learned through experience.

She was right.

As time wore on, I released a lot more books and learned a lot more about the writing, marketing, and publishing process, to the point where I began mentoring and coaching other authors on their manuscripts, then I became a proofreader, then an editor, then I learned formatting, and my skill set continued to grow as time wore on.

Today, I am at the point where I can paint a much fuller picture of all that goes into self-publishing, and my goal is to share the insights I have gained over the years with authors who are in the same boat I was in.

My Journey As A Self-Published Author

Before I published my first book, I did tons of research, yet I still felt like every time I would find answers to some of my questions, new questions arose. It was overwhelming, exciting, frustrating, and frightening all at the same time.

After my first book was published in 2016, I realized the work was only halfway done. After I had successfully produced the book, now it was time to market it and work on another one. A year later, I published my second book, and that was when I realized the world of publishing had changed. Gone were the days when readers expected to wait a full year for new releases. Now, it was more like a release a month, a release every forty-five days, or in some cases, a release every three weeks.

It seemed overwhelming at first, yet exciting, because once my first and second books were published, my mind became flooded with ideas for stories.

As I mentioned previously, along with producing more books, my skill set also increased. I went from not feeling like I knew much at all about self-publishing to becoming an editor, an alpha/beta/test reader, a developmental reviewer, a formatter, a ghostwriter, a publication assistant, and an instructor on book optimization and Amazon ads (more about my courses later!).

In addition to expanding my skill set, I am also a multi-time bestselling and award winning author who writes in multiple genres. It is my hope the insights shared in this book will help other authors reach similar heights or go even higher.

How to Use This Book

This book is divided into multiple chapters, each dedicated to a different focus related to self-publishing: manuscript preparation, manuscript publishing, and manuscript marketing, as well as other tips and tricks that an author can use when they self-publish books. The book does not have to be read in order but reading it in order may be beneficial to an author who feels they have little or no knowledge about self-publishing.

For authors who are more experienced, feel free to bounce around to the topics that are most interesting or informative for you.

For more information related to the concepts covered in this book, feel free to subscribe to my YouTube page, Tanisha Stewart.

See you there!

Tanisha Stewart

Manuscript Preparation

Author Assistance

In addition to editors, formatters, cover designers, and publication assistance, sometimes authors need assistance in other areas. The aforementioned subjects will be covered later, but this section will discuss:
- Writing coaches
- Ghostwriters

Writing Coaches

A writing coach is typically an author and/or editor who demonstrates expertise in crafting stories to the point that he or she can assist other authors in completing their manuscripts for publication. Various writing coaches may structure their sessions in different ways for the authors they are assisting.

For example, when I coach authors, I use a flexible approach based on the author's needs. We work together to draft an outline of the story, then remain on top of the progress via phone call, Zoom meetings, emails, and/or text messages - whatever the author prefers. In addition to this, I also meet with the author on as frequent of a basis as they desire - weekly, biweekly, or monthly. This process continues until the manuscript is complete and ready for publication.

It's important to note that the process I described above is specific to my style of coaching. Other coaches may use a different process. For example, some may want the manuscript to be outlined or completed before they offer coaching, etc. Each coach has their own process, and it's important to the aspiring author to ask about their coach's process before beginning a coaching program.

Ghostwriters

A ghostwriter is typically used for authors who have ideas for a story but don't feel they have the time or skillset to write the story themselves. The ghostwriter writes the story for the author, and the author receives the credit.

Like coaching, ghostwriting can take on different forms. When I ghostwrite for clients, I interview them regarding their desires for the story, then produce an outline. Once the outline is approved, I develop the first draft. Once the first draft is approved, the story is fine-tuned, then prepared for editing, formatting, and publication.

Depending on the options the client chooses, I also obtain an official copyright, ISBN and barcode, hire a cover designer, publish the book in their name, and train them on how to market and/or run ads on their book to ensure success. Other ghostwriters may follow different processes, but many of their approaches may be similar to mine. Ghostwriting can also vary widely in price. Some ghostwriters can charge as little as $500 for a manuscript, while others may charge thousands of dollars. Before choosing a ghostwriter, it is important to ask questions about the process and have a clear understanding of exactly what is included in the package they offer.

Writing

This chapter will focus on various aspects of writing a book. Subjects include:
- character development
- plot development
- perspectives
- outlining

Character Development

One aspect of storytelling that some authors have no problems with, while others seem to struggle, is character development. Most authors can get a clear view of the main character of their book but have trouble fleshing out the character and making him or her multidimensional. When it comes to side characters, this can also be a struggle. The following are some tips on character development.

First, try to narrow down how many characters you want in a book. Technically, a book can have as many characters as you'd like, but it is better to have a book with less characters who are all well-rounded than it is to have a book with too many characters to the point that it becomes confusing.

I am guilty of writing some stories with many characters in them. What I did with those stories was create storylines for each character that were unique and distinct from the main character and other characters. These characters had to play some sort of major role in the story to be included.

It's best if every character in the story is connected to the main character or characters in some significant way. Otherwise, it might be best to exclude them. I had to do this in one story I wrote called

<u>When Things Go Left</u>. In that story, there were four main characters, and one of the main characters originally had three cousins who would play critical roles in his story arc. However, my editor suggested there were too many characters and that readers might become confused, so I merged some traits of his third cousin into the other two, so now the main character had two cousins. This worked well because they had distinct personalities that readers were easily able to distinguish.

Another aspect of character development is the character's voice. How does this character think? How would he or she react to various situations? What makes him or her different from the other characters in the book? What is his or her backstory? All this information needs to be known by you, the author. However, all of it does not need to be told to the reader. The most critical parts of each character's backgrounds and traits should shine through as the story unfolds.

Each character should have some type of major conflict, as well as a few minor conflicts that contribute to the major conflict. The protagonist, or central character of the book, also needs to have a goal they are trying to reach, but some kind of obstacle in their way that hinders or makes it seemingly impossible to accomplish their objective.

For example, another story I wrote entitled [For My Good: My Baby Daddy Ain't Ish](), the main character's major conflict was her son's father and his volatile attitude toward her and their child. Her minor conflicts included a drinking problem, financial issues, difficulty with school, and stress on her job, as well as internal conflict about a budding relationship with another man. Each of these minor conflicts were in some way influenced by her major conflict with her son's father. As the story unfolded, the character navigated each of these issues until she reached her climactic and ending points. This story was also part of a series, and the character's development continued, adding and removing other sources of conflict, many of which were related to her son's father until the finale, where all issues were resolved.

Character development can be both a challenging and fun process. The most important things to remember are to make sure the characters are unique, relatable, realistic, and well-rounded with a balanced set of conflicts. This will keep readers reading and lead to stronger attachments between the reader and the story.

Plot Development

Just like characters need to be well developed, the plot of a story needs to be well developed. Developing the plot of a story becomes easier with using an outline in many cases, which will be discussed in a later section. One of the biggest issues some authors face is plot holes or inconsistencies in their stories. Because this is a significant issue for some authors, the following are some tips on how to ensure plot holes and inconsistencies are eliminated from your story.

The first is to map the story out. This is easier if the author used an outline to develop the manuscript, because all one would have to do is examine the outline and ensure that everything adds up, no loose ends are left untied, and that all timelines and storylines blend cohesively. If the author did not use an outline and just wrote the story as it came to them, this is also fine. I would suggest either reading the story back over and mapping out critical points as you go to ensure the flow is progressing smoothly or developing a rough sketch of what happened in the story during each chapter, then studying the sketch to look for holes or inconsistencies. Were all questions answered? Does anything not line up? If so, go back and correct any issues you catch, and the flow of the story should improve.

Another method is using alpha, beta, or test readers. These types of readers will be discussed in greater detail in a later section, but to provide a quick definition, these readers are individuals who will read your story before it is released (sometimes before it is edited or proofread) and provide feedback to see if they saw any errors or inconsistencies. Although it's not a requirement, it is a wise idea to have someone look over a book before it is sent to an editor to uncover and possibly resolve major issues that may exist. It is best to have more than one person go through your story, but even having just one person will still help tremendously if the individual you choose is trustworthy to provide an honest opinion and thorough examination of the story. The term *trustworthy* in this context can have a range of meanings, but for the purposes of vetting a manuscript, a trustworthy reader is someone who avidly reads in the genre the book is written in, is knowledgeable about story structure, and who is willing to provide specific feedback on the manuscript. To help this process, the author can provide a short list of elements for the reader to focus on as they read, then ask for feedback on those elements, or the author can ask questions about these elements after feedback is already provided. The idea behind this is to eliminate problem areas and make the manuscript the most presentable it can be before it is sent to an editor or published.

The final method is to send your story to an editor. There are different types of editors, which will be discussed in more detail in a later section, but the type of editor you would be looking for in this scenario is a developmental editor. A developmental editor's job is to look for things like plot holes and inconsistencies and provide guidance on how they can be resolved.

Perspectives

Another aspect of writing is deciding whether your story should be written in first person or third person, and then deciding which type of first or third person narrative you should provide. For some authors, this decision is made by looking at other books in his or her genre and seeing what the most popular or bestselling authors are doing. Another way to make the decision is to let the story speak to you. Are the characters speaking to you directly? If so, then a first-person narrative might be best.

If the characters aren't necessarily speaking to you, but you see their story unfolding, a third person narrative might be best. Some authors prefer to write all their stories in one perspective - this is fine. Some readers only read books written from a certain perspective - this is also fine.

For me as an author, I like to switch it up and write some books in first person narrative and others in third person narrative. I believe it helps me sharpen my skill set, and my opinion is that some stories are best told in one perspective, while others are best told in the other. The following is a brief explanation of each, as well as the various subcategories associated with them.

The first-person narrative can be broken up into two basic categories: having one main character narrate the entire book from his or her perspective or having multiple characters share their points of view. I have written both types of books. When Things Go Left, a book I mentioned previously, was a multi-POV first person narrative. For My Good: My Baby Daddy Ain't Ish, however, was a first-person narrative told from one character's point of view.

The third person narrative can be broken into multiple categories as well. The two main categories are third person omniscient and third person limited. These two categories can be confusing for many authors, including myself at times, but the basic difference is that a third person omniscient point of view is when the narrator speaks from a top-down level, knows all information about all characters and narrates it in an unbiased manner (not positively or negatively skewing reader's perceptions), while third person limited is when the story is still told in third person, but one character's perspective is narrated per scene or chapter. An example of a third person limited novel that I have written is Even Me, Full Circle. A Third person omniscient story I've written is Should Have Thought Twice.

Some authors like to play with perspectives and do a combination of both, with some parts of their stories told in third person, while the other parts are told in first person. In my opinion, this can be done, as long as it doesn't confuse the reader. One story I've done this with is When Things Go Left. The prologue of the story is written during the main character's childhoods, so it is told in third person, while the rest of the story is a first person, multi-POV story.

Outlining

When it comes to the subject of outlining, there are various ways to do so. Some authors outline all their books, while some outline some of their books or parts of their books, and others don't outline at all.

There are three basic ways to outline: providing a rough sketch of the book, outlining chapter by chapter, and outlining scene by scene. As you can imagine, each level of outlining gets deeper and deeper and becomes more and more complex.

The easiest one to describe is the rough sketch of a book. This is the simplest form of outlining because essentially all the author is doing is coming up with the beginning, climactic point(s), and ending of a story. Once these are developed, the author has a basic idea of what he or she wants the story to be about and the direction it is going. It makes the story easier to start, build, and finish.

The second form of outlining goes a little deeper. A chapter by chapter outline lets the author know roughly how long the book is going to be because the chapters are set beforehand. For instance, if the author is shooting for a full-length novel, he or she will probably have more chapters than if the author is trying to write a short story. In this type of outline, the author provides a brief statement of what will happen in each chapter of the story. This provides an even clearer map of the overall story because the author can target potential problem areas or parts where the story might lag or even figure out if certain chapters need to be added or eliminated. It can help a story move at a smoother place than a rough sketch outline because the author knows exactly where he or she is going at all times with the story.

The final form of outlining is a scene by scene outline. In this form of writing, the author literally maps out each scene of the book within each chapter, sometimes even including specific quotes the characters will say to each other, locations they will be, etc. This is the most detailed version of an outline. It is so thorough that if the author chose to sell it to someone else, the other person would be able to create the entire story by themselves using what the selling author has written. This type of outline makes for the smoothest form of writing because the entire story is basically already written. The author simply has to flesh out the scenes based on what is described. That being said it is important to note that this form of outline takes a great deal of time and dedication.

One final note about outlining is that with each level, the story becomes easier to write, but sometimes with even the most complex outlines, the characters may decide to go in a different direction. In this case, sometimes small tweaks can be made to the rest of the outline, but other times, an author may have to completely revise their outline. This isn't necessarily a bad thing, but it is something to take note of for those who may have this happen and become discouraged as a result.

Editing

Just as there are various ways one can write a book, there are several ways in which a book can be edited. This section will discuss four different forms of editing:
- Developmental
- Self-editing
- Copy/line editing
- Proofreading

Before we begin this discussion, it's important to note the topic of editing can be quite controversial for a number of reasons. One of the reasons is that some authors believe hiring an editor is absolutely necessary and that no story can truly be successful or well written without one, while others believe hiring an editor is a good idea but not necessary if one has the right tools that would replace what an editor does.

I fall somewhere in the middle. I've had some books where I felt like I needed an editor to help me sort out some issues, and I've written some books and edited them myself. In both cases, I've seen success and positive reviews. It all boils down to one's budget, their skillset, how well the story and characters are crafted, and how strategic one is in their marketing and publication process.

Let's discuss developmental editing, self-editing, copy/line editing, and proofreading in turn.

Developmental Editing

As previously discussed, a developmental editor is one who helps to improve the flow, plot, and character development of the story and who helps to ensure it is well written and no stones are left unturned. A good developmental editor has a sharp eye for detail, character voice, and plot trajectory.

With feedback from a developmental editor, one should see lots of comments in the margins or otherwise about how the story is moving, whether the characters are well developed, whether there are any holes in the plot, and whether there are any areas of the manuscript that need to be rewritten or removed. A developmental editor will also discuss whether the story is lacking anything in its development. This may mean the author needs to add more to the story or make changes in the story's structure. If you are a first-time author or an author with limited experience in plot development and other areas of writing, I would suggest a developmental editor.

One thing to note is a developmental editor is also the highest form of editing, so it will cost the most in most cases. That being said it's still a wise investment for those who wish to turn a good book into a great story.

Self-Editing

The next topic is somewhat controversial. In a sense, every author does some form of self-editing because all authors read their stories at least once to ensure what they wrote comes across in the way they intended. The level of self-editing individual authors engage in is a different story. Some authors do extensive self-editing where they break their story down chapter by chapter, focus on one at a time, have a computer program read the story back to them, and use outside programs like Grammerly and ProWriting Aid to assist in the development of the story.

Authors who have a good eye for detail, character and plot development, and flow can probably do a self-edit on their books and have them ready for publication by the end of the process. Some would argue that even if the author is strong in the areas I mentioned they still need another set of eyes on their manuscript.

I wouldn't disagree with that notion, I would only argue that in terms of the success of the manuscript, positive reviews received, and reader engagement, it's not a hundred percent necessary. When in doubt, especially as a newer author, I would not recommend solely using self-editing for a manuscript.

Copy/Line Editing

The next forms of editing to be discussed are copy and line editing. Copyediting involves resolving issues with grammar, punctuation, syntax, and other technical areas involved with writing. It requires a strong attention to detail and a solid knowledge base of the mechanics of writing.

Line editing is similar to copyediting, except it goes deeper. Line editing focuses on the manuscript on a sentence by sentence level, focusing on the style the manuscript is written in, as well as the flow and pacing of the storyline. A line editor will tighten up the way the story is written by removing or rearranging sentences that need work, making shorter, punchier lines where needed, and eliminating lines in the manuscript which are unnecessary or redundant to paint a clearer picture for the reader.

A copy edit, like developmental editing, is a wise choice for any author, even those who already have a keen eye for these types of details. As with developmental editing, it's not a hundred percent necessary, but I would argue that its value would make it worth the investment.

Proofreading

Proofreading is considered the lowest form of editing, but it is a powerful tool that every writer should use. Proofreading is similar to copyediting in that the manuscript is checked for errors in spelling, capitalization, punctuation, and the like, but the main difference is that proofreading is typically the last form of editing that is done before the book is published and sent to the masses.

I would highly recommend a proofread even if an author has opted out of developmental, copy or line editing because it will at least ensure that there are minimal or no errors in a story to improve quality and clarity. One thing to consider is that some proofreaders have a threshold they stick to in terms of how many errors they will edit before they decide the book requires a copy or line edit before it is proofread. Some proofreaders also do not accept a book at all if it has not been line or copyedited. Neither of the aforementioned are bad things for the aspiring author. After all, if a book is riddled with errors, it is highly likely that even an expert proofreader will not be able to catch them all. It is also an indication that the story needs developmental editing in addition to copy or line editing. I believe that if an author finds him or herself in this position, it's likely worth it to invest more funds into hiring a developmental or line/copy editor before a proofreader. We all want our books to shine.

A Final Note

As one can imagine, it is tough for a lot of authors to find editors who are not only reputable but who will do a thorough job. Here are some recommendations for editors that I have either heard of or worked with in the past. I offer editing services and can be contacted at tanishastewart.author@gmail.com.

The first recommended editor is Cyn Anne at the Cynful Monarch. I have hired Cyn to edit multiple books for me, and each experience was professional, timely, and high quality. The books that Cyn has edited for me have all done well - one became a number one bestseller in my category, one became my highest selling book of all time and won an award, and two others were nominated for awards.

Other editors who I have not worked with personally but have heard good things about are Bianca Shakur at b.edits and Adrienne Horn at I A.M. Editing, Ink.

Formatting

The next topic to be discussed has to do with the visual display of the manuscript. Formatting for eBooks versus paperbacks or hardcover books will have some differences, but the overall goal for both is to provide a look and feel for your book that is professional. Authors include things like copyright pages, author's notes, acknowledgement pages, links and descriptions for subsequent novels, and the like. The goal of formatting is to incorporate whichever of these elements you choose in a manner that is standardized.

For example, the most basic formatting might include a title page, copyright page, table of contents, half title page, manuscript, then author catalog.

The following sections will discuss some differences in formatting when it comes to various forms of the book, including:

- eBooks
- Paperbacks and hardcovers
- Simple formatting versus advanced formatting

eBooks

Formatting for eBooks is arguably easier than paperbacks or hardcovers because devices like Kindles and cell phones allow readers the flexibility to choose how they want their books displayed. They can choose to change the background colors, enlarge the font, and do other things to customize their reading experience.

Because of this, if there is a page break in between each of the above-mentioned parts of a formatted eBook, the display will come across as professional to the reader.

Paperbacks and Hardcovers

Paperbacks and hardcovers have more strict guidelines when it comes to formatting. Some of these guidelines include font styles, font sizes, whether to include a table of contents, and size of the book. When it comes to font styles, it's best to use a serif or sans serif font to ensure the reader has an easier experience. A serif or sans serif font is one that does not have extensions at the ends of letters, which makes for a cleaner read.

When it comes to font sizes, it's best to use a size that will be easier to read. Choosing an 8 or 9 size font might cause some readers to strain

Cover Design

This next section will discuss various aspects of cover design, including:
- how to choose cover elements
- selecting a cover designer

Cover Elements

The first thing any author should do is conduct research on the Top 100 list of whichever genre(s) they are writing in to ensure their book will look similar to the covers that are displayed. I am not suggesting authors copy covers from the Top 100 list, but that they look for commonalities in things like font sizes and styles, cover models/stock images, and color schemes. Once the author has a solid understanding of what the top selling books in their genre look like, they will be able to direct their cover designer in how their own cover should be structured.

Some designers offer premade covers, which can make the process easier for multiple reasons. First, premade covers are usually less expensive than customized covers. Second, if the author finds themselves having trouble deciding exactly how they want their cover to look, a premade cover could be a source of inspiration.

Lastly, if the author needs the cover in a quick timeframe, having a premade cover makes the process much smoother. Premade covers can be found on many designer's websites and social media groups, as well as other sites that sell covers.

Choosing a Cover Designer

If the aspiring author is not well connected in the publishing community, they may feel like finding a cover designer will be an impossible feat. I remember feeling like this when I was searching for a cover designer for my debut novel, Even Me.

I found my designer by conducting an internet search and typing the name of my genre + cover designer. After much searching, I found a comment on a blog site which mentioned the name of a cover designer. I visited the designer's website and sent her an email. She ended up designing fourteen of my covers.

Speaking of cover designers and how to find them, I have some great suggestions based on designers I have worked with in the past. One is Tyora Moody of Tywebbin Creations. She designed my Even Me, When Things Go, and For My Good series covers. Another is Iesha Bree of IBDesignz. She designed one of my top selling books of all time, A Husband, a Boyfriend, & a Side Dude, plus multiple others.

Lastly, Karie Walker at The Cover Stalker. She has designed all my thriller covers, including my infamous story, Everybody Ain't Your Friend, which has been my highest selling book to date. Each of these cover designers does an outstanding job, and Tyora and Karie's covers helped to land me at the number one spot in the best seller's lists for my genres. There are multiple other cover designers out there as well. Fiverr.com is a site where there are various designers who do great work.

Whichever route an author chooses, he or she should be sure to vet their designers to ensure they are legitimate and will do quality work. The vetting process should include questions about stock photos and licensing for images, whether the designer offers both eBook and paperback designs, pricing, etc. If the designer does not display examples of their work on their sites or social media pages, ask for examples of their work. Ask other authors who they use for cover design. Choosing a cover designer can be tough but also fun.

Making it "Official"

Three other elements help to make an author's books more official and boost credibility. The first is registering their books with official copyrights. The second is obtaining an ISBN. The third is pursuing an LLC. Each of these options will be discussed in turn in the following sections.

Registering a Copyright

The first thing to note is that whenever a person writes, types, or emails any form of creative or intellectual documentation, that documentation is automatically copyrighted. Basic copyright laws state that anything we create automatically belongs to us.

That being said, when it comes to registering an official copyright, it may be beneficial for an author to do this because the official register will help make the process easier if he or she runs into issues with plagiarism. An unofficial copyright can still stand in the court of law, but an official copyright will help to cut time and costs down significantly. An official copyright can be obtained at copyright.gov, and the cost at the time of this publication is $65 USD.

Obtaining an ISBN and Barcode

There are multiple ways an author can obtain an ISBN, both officially and unofficially. Unofficially, most platforms that offer the opportunity for self-publishing also provide the author with a free ISBN and barcode. The ISBN serves as a unique tracking number to an author's books so it's easily searchable. The barcode contains sales information such as the price of the book. The main reason that using a free ISBN is considered "unofficial" is because if the author decides to upload their paperback to multiple sites, there will be multiple ISBNs floating around with the same title. This could create potential issues with one or more platforms accusing the author of plagiarism, and it can also cause the author to lose credibility in the eyes of some readers. If an author chooses to exclusively publish their books with one company, this won't be a problem, but if he or she ever wants to publish on multiple platforms or offer his or her book in bookstores, having an official ISBN will make the process a lot smoother.

Officially, ISBNs are sold on bowker.com. The cost for a single ISBN and barcode at the time of this publication is $150 USD ($125 for the ISBN and $25 for the barcode). Purchasing an official ISBN will allow authors to have a single unique code attached to their books so they can universally be found using this number.

If an author wishes to have their books sold at bookstores, offered at libraries, and published to multiple platforms, I would highly recommend obtaining an ISBN.

Pursuing an LLC

An LLC is a business license. It establishes the author as a brand and boosts credibility. It also offers certain protections and perks. Regarding protections, if the author runs into any legal issues such as a lawsuit, the author him or herself would not be liable for potential damages, they would be assigned to the company.

Also, establishing an LLC can help in other areas, like if an author wants to sell merchandise associated with their books or brand. In addition to this, many authors pursue an LLC to obtain business credit to help cover the costs associated with publishing their books. Lastly, some authors choose to pursue an LLC because they wish to own a publishing company, either solely for their books or for other author's books who they sign to their company.

Obtaining an LLC can be beneficial depending on an author's goals. To learn more, an author should visit their local small business center.

Manuscript Publishing

Platforms

There are multiple platforms where an author can publish his or her books, including Amazon, Barnes and Noble, Kobo, Ingram Sparks, Lulu, and others, including the author's own website. For the purposes of this book, we will focus on the ins and outs of publishing on Amazon. The reason for this is Amazon hosts the majority of readers, making it the largest online book retailer. Various aspects of publishing on Amazon will be discussed, including:
- Kindle Unlimited
- Expanded Distribution
- Audible
- Kindle Vella

Kindle Unlimited

Amazon hosts a sub-platform called Kindle Unlimited (KU). KU is essentially designed to work like Netflix, except it's used for books. Readers can borrow a certain number of books at a time, read them, and return them for other books. Authors are paid for every page that is read in their books.

Whether an author should put their books on KU is a matter of controversy for many self-publishers. It largely boils down to the author's goals, genre, and publishing strategy to make the correct choice for their books. We will briefly discuss some of the pros and cons.

Pros of Publishing via KU

There are arguably a lot of pros for publishing eBooks via KU. For example, along with Amazon being the largest book retailer, and therefore holding most of the market, KU is also an extremely popular avenue used by avid readers who don't have a large budget but like to read. With KU, they can borrow, read, and switch as many books as they would like in each month, all for the same nominal fee. The cost effectiveness is astronomical. For authors, this works well, too - many authors earn the bulk of their royalties from the KU program.

Another pro is that enrolling a book in KU does not prohibit an author from charging whichever price they choose for direct sales of their eBooks. This in effect provides an additional stream of income - one for direct eBook sales, and one for eBooks read via KU. Sales on both sides can add up quickly for an author, which can help to produce future books more efficiently by increasing one's budget.

Lastly, enrolling in KU may be a good idea for authors because some readers are "KU exclusive", meaning that they don't buy eBooks directly at all - they solely use KU for their literary needs. This is an important thing to note for self-published authors.

My suggestion is to use KU, especially as an aspiring or new author, to build a reader base. If an author does not like KU, he or she can always unenroll (and later re-enroll, if he or she chooses) after ninety days for any given eBook.

Cons of Publishing via KU

Although there are certainly pros of publishing via KU, and I recommend using this route, there are a few caveats as well. First, if an author chooses to publish their eBook via KU, he or she is bound to have that eBook solely published on Amazon with the exclusion of any other eBook retailer. In other words, an author who uses KU is not allowed to *go wide* or publish their eBook on other platforms outside of Amazon. This is certainly something to consider, especially if the author writes in a genre that does well when it is widely published. It also will play a role if the author has a desire to sell an eBook directly from his or her website. Selling from one's own website would be prohibited if enrolled in KU.

Another downside of publishing via KU is the payout fluctuates every month. Kindle Unlimited relies on a fund that Amazon sets aside each month, and because it fluctuates, this can mean a difference of hundreds of dollars each month with authors sometimes earning hundreds of dollars more for the same amount of sales they may earn hundreds of dollars less for another month. This is certainly something to consider, especially if an author's genre does not sale well in KU. It may be more beneficial for authors who fit this category to go wide with their books rather than remaining exclusive to Amazon.

Doing Both?

One final thing I would like to note about KU is that authors can technically do both for any given eBook. What I mean by this is an author could potentially leave their books in

KU for a given timeframe, then take their book out of KU and go wide for a while, then put the book back in KU, etc. This is a sales strategy used by many authors who have studied how their sales fluctuate when using KU versus going wide.

Another strategy is to enroll the eBook in KU for the first ninety days after it releases, then take it out and go wide for the remainder of its time. This strategy has proven effective for some authors who have seen a large boost in sales that carries them over into other platforms they choose to publish their eBook on.

Expanded Distribution

Paperbacks also have options to earn additional streams of income. Amazon hosts a program called Expanded Distribution, which allows for sales of an author's books at a discounted rate through third party retailers. The author is paid a smaller royalty, but the legwork involved with placing his or her books on these other platforms him or herself is done away with. Of course, Amazon does not advertise books on all platforms, but having a few extra options only helps sales.

Audible

In addition to having a paperback, hardcover, or eBook, Amazon also allows authors to sell audiobooks on their platform. Acx.com is the site that can be used to find narrators or upload files the author has narrated him or herself. There are a few different options for getting an audiobook published. First, the author can narrate themselves, as mentioned before. Second, the author can hire a narrator directly from ACX by posting the book for auditions or sending a direct offer. Lastly, authors can hire outside narrators from personal websites or sites like fiverr.com and upload the files when the work is completed.

For an author who is just starting out, I would suggest either narrating oneself or hiring a narrator through ACX. One thing to note about narrating oneself is that narrating takes a great deal of time, and the editing process for audiobook narration takes even longer than the recording process. Also, ACX has strict requirements for audio levels, etc, so special equipment and training is highly recommended if an author chooses this route. Although more expensive than self-narration, hiring a narrator can make for a much smoother process. The reason for this is that ACX has safeguards in place to ensure fairness for both the narrator and the author that may not be available if using other avenues.

In addition to being able to hire a narrator through ACX, there are also multiple payment options: royalty share, royalty share plus, and paying upfront. The royalty share option allows for authors to pay no money up front but to split the royalties from the audiobook each month with their narrator. This means a significant pay cut because ACX takes sixty percent of royalties, so the author and narrator would receive twenty percent each. The royalty share plus option is much like royalty share, except the author agrees to an additional upfront payment along with splitting royalties. Lastly, paying upfront means the author keeps the full forty percent of their royalties.

Each of these options can be beneficial to authors depending on their goals and budget, but I would recommend paying upfront so the author does not have to share their royalties.

One final note is that in order to gain the full forty percent of royalties, the author also has to enroll their audiobook exclusively in Amazon audible. If the author chooses to publish their audiobook on multiple platforms, the royalty percentage decreases.

Kindle Vella

The last sub-platform I would like to discuss is Kindle Vella. Kindle Vella is a program Amazon uses for authors who enjoy writing serial fiction. What is serial fiction? Essentially, it is writing a story in episodes, where readers unlock one episode at a time. Authors are paid for each episode that is read, as well as a bonus for each new reader they bring to the program. There are pros and cons to Kindle Vella, which will be discussed in turn.

Pros of Kindle Vella

The first pro to using Kindle Vella is that it provides the opportunity for authors to try out new pen names and genres in a low-risk manner. If readers aren't tuning into a story after a few episodes, the author can discard it. If readers are tuning in, the author has good data in his or her hands. He or she can discover which episodes are most read, most liked, and most reviewed. This can help strengthen writing and marketing strategy, as well as help to develop the plot.

Another pro is that once the story is officially complete, after thirty days, the author can release it as a paperback, eBook, and hardcover on kdp.com, as well as an audiobook on acx.com. This provides an additional source of income for authors on top of the others that already exist.

Cons of Kindle Vella

There are also downsides to Kindle Vella. The first is that it can be difficult to find readers. Because it is a different platform, readers who enjoy an author's books on the main Amazon site may not crossover into Kindle Vella. This may make the author feel like they have to rebuild their readership from the ground up. Also, many readers complain that they do not like serial fiction. Of course, this is not true for all readers because there is a large market for readers of serial fiction, but it is important to note for authors who have not produced stories in this manner in the past.

Manuscript Marketing

Building a Team

Another important aspect of book writing is building a launch team. The launch team can include individuals like other authors who write in similar genres promoting your book or even paid promoters. In addition to this, it is helpful for authors to have alpha readers, beta readers, review teams, participate in review sites, and host an email list. A quick note about alpha and beta readers: it is a good idea to have a contract in place to protect your work from potential plagiarism, etc. Also, while many readers provide these services for free, some do charge for their time and dedication.

Alpha Readers

An alpha reader (sometimes referred to as a test reader) is a person who reads all or parts of a story either during the process of writing or after the first draft is finished. An alpha/test reader sees the story in its rawest form and is allowed to give feedback the author can use before sending a more finalized draft to an editor.

Beta Readers

Beta readers, also sometimes referred to as test readers, are individuals who read a book after it is completed but before it is published. These readers see the edited version of the book and offer final feedback on certain aspects of the story that may need to be enhanced or tweaked before publication. Beta readers also may prepare a review for the book that they will post on release day.

Review Teams

A review team is a group of individuals who read the final version of a book, either before or after it is published, and leave their reviews on or shortly after the release day. When using a review team, it is best for authors to have reviewers stagger their reviews with some leaving reviews on the first day of release and others leaving their reviews in the days following the release, up to a week.

With this strategy, it's best to have a large team (a hundred would be ideal or as many as the author can obtain).

Review Sites

Another element to the author's launch team could involve the use of review sites. There are various sites, such as Booksprout, which allow authors to post advance copies of their books in hopes that he or she will gain new readers and increase the number of reviews.

Email List

Last but not least, having an email list can be extremely helpful to increase sales, reviews, and exposure for an author's books. With a targeted email list full of avid readers who enjoy the author's books, the author can find it much easier to reach the Top 100 list, or even the best seller's list, for their books. Email lists are a powerful tool, and they are worth looking into.

Marketing

After the book is completed and published, the author must market it if he or she wants to help ensure financial success or make a profit. There are various avenues for marketing a book, and because there are so many, they all will not be covered in this book. This chapter will focus on social media, book signings, author websites, amazon ads, Bookbub ads, developing a marketing strategy, reader magnets, and paid promoters and promotion sites.

Social Media

There are many social media sources that various authors have found useful in their marketing endeavors. The great thing is that an author does not have to use them all. He or she can decide which ones they are most comfortable with, learn how they work, and use them as their focus. It's advised to market this way to avoid spreading oneself too thin. Once an author reaches a certain level of financial success, he or she may be able to hire a marketing or social media manager to handle the daily tasks associated with managing various forms of social media. Let's discuss some of them in turn.

Facebook

Because of its popularity, almost everyone in the United States has a Facebook account. This includes authors as well as other entrepreneurs. Authors can create business pages for their brand, run Facebook advertisements, pay a fee to have their individual posts spread to various audiences, and more. Facebook marketing, as with any other form of marketing, can be a challenge, but some authors have seen great success using this tool.

Instagram

Instagram is another great tool which allows authors to post pictures and videos related to their books. Hashtags become extremely important when using Instagram, so I would suggest that an author learns more about how hashtags work, as well as which hashtags to use to assist them in their journey. Another great thing about Instagram is that if an author's Facebook page is connected to their Instagram account, he or she can run ads from one platform, but have them show up on both Facebook and Instagram. This is a nice way to target a wide span of readers.

Twitter

Twitter is another largely popular avenue for authors to market their books. Twitter users post tweets - short messages of 280 characters or less - to their audiences, and these messages can contain links to articles and videos and can include pictures as well. Tweets can be retweeted or shared, which will help the author reach a wider audience. Twitter also has dedicated groups who focus on a range of genres.

TikTok

TikTok is an ever-growing platform where authors can post video, voiceover, and musical content associated with their books. Examples include live readings, giveaways, quotes, videos of authors flipping the pages of their books, authors portraying characters in their books, and more. TikTok is a highly creative platform that can lead to great success for any author, especially if his or her content goes viral.

Reader Groups

Reader groups can be hosted across various platforms, including author's email lists, Facebook, Twitter, and author websites. Regardless of the platform or avenue an author chooses to host his or her reader's group, providing meaningful interactions and content is best. If the author develops a solid connection with his or her audience, this can help with successful book launches, gaining reviews, and more.

Blogs

Some authors have a specific passion or focus they are interested in that provides enough content to use in a blog. Blogs can be produced daily, weekly, or even monthly, though the more frequent options are suggested. Blogs can focus on a range of topics both book-related and unrelated to books. Either way, blogs can be a powerful tool to market one's books.

Book Signings

Another method authors can use to market their books is book signings. Book signings can be hosted from various sources, such as book clubs, bookstores, author vending events, mixed vending events, and events not related to books. Regardless of the avenue, authors can use book signings to connect with new readers or to meet up with existing readers. Authors can set themselves up for success by providing a professional experience, giving away small items like bookmarks, excerpts from books, and more.

Author Websites

Another avenue authors can use to market their books is their website. An author can use his or her websites to sell merchandise related to their books, sell eBooks, paperbacks, and audiobooks directly, as well as host blogs, email lists, and reader's groups. Author websites can set writers up for success by providing a professional appearance and boosting credibility.

Amazon Ads

Amazon ads are another highly effective tool for authors. There are multiple types of Amazon ads that can be run, including automatic ads, where Amazon targets prospective readers based on an author's previous reader history, similar books based on the genre their books are in, and more. Other types of ads include keyword ads and category ads. Amazon ads are highly effective in that they can help an author boost sales tremendously and sustain a passive income. When I started running Amazon Ads on my books, the first month I earned five times my highest monthly income, and that number has been increasing ever since.

Bookbub Ads

Bookbub is one of the leading sites for readers and authors because it hosts a huge email list that targets readers of multiple genres. As a result, authors have the potential to reach large numbers of readers all at once when they run ads on this platform. In addition to running Bookbub ads, there are also Bookbub featured deals, which is a highly competitive option that allows author's books to be selected as featured books for a specific timeframe. Landing a Bookbub featured deal has led many authors to huge success, sometimes with thousands of downloads and hundreds of reviews.

Reader Magnets

Another option that may be helpful as a marketing tool is for an author to use reader magnets. Reader magnets can take on a few different forms, but essentially, a reader magnet is free content. This can be a chapter, short story, bonus scene, or full-length novel, whichever the author chooses. Some authors have multiple reader magnets, but the idea is for the reader magnets to draw more readers to the author's paid books. Reader magnets can be offered in exchange for signing up for an author's email list, or they can be offered in the form of permafree books. A permafree book is a book that is offered for free on Amazon. Typically, it is the first or third book in a series, or it can be a prequel to a series. Permafree books are designed to draw readers in and lead to increased sales on paid books.

Paid Promoters

Sometimes authors would rather have someone else promote their books on social media to help gain a following or increase sales. There are lots of paid promoters on various platforms like Facebook and Instagram, and for some authors, this option can be helpful. One promoter I would recommend is Brandie Davis-White, founder of the My Urban Books Club 2.0 on Facebook. She offers paid promotion at a low price, but it can yield a significant increase in an author's sales and/or visibility.

Promotion Sites

Last but not least, there are free and paid promotion sites an author can use to promote their books. These sites are most helpful during a book launch but can be helpful at any time to boost visibility and sales.

Developing a Strategy

Whichever route an author chooses to market their books, the best bet is to use a strategy. Some options, such as running Amazon Ads, don't take a great deal of planning to execute, but others, such as social media marketing and Bookbub ads, will likely require an author to develop a schedule for the content they plan to produce associated with their book. I would suggest that authors try all the options above over time. Take note of which ones work best for your books and genres and develop skills in those areas. This will help to maximize time and energy in your author journey.

Publishing

There are multiple ways an author can publish his or her books. There are pros and cons to each method. The methods and their pros and cons will be discussed in the following sections.

Self-Publishing

A person who self publishes his or her books retains full rights and control to their books. Self-publishing a book is easy. All an author needs are a manuscript, cover, and kdp account to publish on Amazon. Because the author retains full control of their book using this method, they also reap the full royalties from their books.

That being said, there are a few cons to self-publishing. The first is that all the work has to be done by the author unless they hire someone to manage their social media, website, marketing, advertising, finding cover designers, finding editors and formatters, and everything else that goes into sustaining sales on their books. If the author has enough in their budget to outsource all or most of the tasks associated with maintaining book sales, he or she is in an ideal position. Otherwise, the author will have to take care of all these responsibilities him or herself. This is doable (I do it!) but it can be time and energy consuming at times.

Vanity Publishers

Vanity Publishers are publishing companies who agree to publish an author's books for a fee. Fees can range from hundreds to thousands of dollars. In addition to that, the vanity publisher may take additional royalties out of an author's books for their services. Publishing through this method is relatively easy, but the obvious drawback is the high cost as well as allowing one's royalties to be split. In addition to this, authors may run into issues with scamming when they come across vanity publishers. Some companies have been known to steal royalties, not produce what they offered to authors in their publishing package, and more. If an author chooses this route, it is best to thoroughly vet the vanity publisher before deciding to sign a contract with them.

There are some positive sides to vanity publishing, however. If the vanity publisher is reputable, it has connections to various marketing opportunities that authors may not have had access to on their own. Some vanity publishers have direct access for their authors to be featured in blogs, interviews, magazines, bookstores, and the like. Vanity publishers also sometimes offer opportunities for book signings and other perks. There is a range of possibilities when it comes to vanity publishers, so again, I would advise authors to thoroughly vet the company and read through the contract carefully to ascertain exactly what is offered.

Indie Publishers

Indie publishers can be like vanity publishers in that some of them charge an upfront fee to authors in exchange for publishing their books in addition to retaining a portion of an author's royalties. Other indie publishers charge no fee, only take a portion of royalties, and lastly, some indie publishers offer authors an advance for their books similar to that of traditional publishers (discussed in the next section).

As with vanity publishing, authors need to thoroughly vet indie publishers to ensure the company they are working with is legitimate. In addition to this, the author needs to ensure they carefully read the contract to see what is offered and required.

Some positive sides to signing with an indie publisher is that some indie publishers offer the same opportunities mentioned above as vanity publishers. In addition to this, both vanity and indie publishers may have access to huge mailing lists of fans in whatever genres they publish, so the author may launch their career with huge success.

If the author signs with a reputable indie publisher, there aren't many drawbacks, however, there are a few things to consider. The first is that typically the indie publisher requires the author to produce a specific number of books over a set timeframe. If the author cannot meet these obligations, they could run into issues. Secondly, even if the author meets all obligations of the indie publisher, he or she is bound to the contract until it ends, meaning if there are issues in the relationship, the author may be stuck without rights to their books and have to wait until they get their rights back before they make changes, unpublish, or republish their books. Next, sometimes indie publishers only allow authors to publish books under their company during the time the author is contracted with them. This may cause issues for an author who wants to write in other genres or self-publish some of their books. Lastly, as with vanity publishing, there have been numerous reports of scamming in the indie publishing community. It is largely an integrity-based system, so be sure to thoroughly vet an indie publisher before going this route.

Traditional Publishers

Traditional publishers are also known as mainstream publishers. Think of names like Penguin Books or Random House. Traditional publishing is the toughest route for authors because it is a highly competitive process. The author needs an agent and query letters to have the opportunity to be considered, and in most cases, they are not considered for publication. There are countless stories about authors receiving hundreds of rejection letters from traditional publishing companies.

If offered an opportunity with a traditional publisher, the author is typically paid an advance for their books. The advance is taken out of their royalties until it is paid off, but if the book doesn't sell well, the author may run into issues with having to pay back part of their advance. On the positive side, traditional publishers offer authors lots of exposure they may not have access to as a self-published or indie published author. This can help ensure financial success in many cases.

When it comes to marketing and advertising, sometimes the author is left to do this themselves, as with indie, vanity, or self-publishing, but sometimes the traditional publisher will offer this as part of their package. Some indie and vanity publishers offer this as well. As always, the author needs to critically examine the contract to see what their responsibilities are and what the publisher is willing to offer.

Finding Your Audience

If you've been an author for any length of time, you've probably been advised to find your audience. What does it mean to find your audience? One definition is to find the characteristics of the demographic your books will best serve. Is it women over forty, or is it teens who are headed to college? The possibilities are endless, and it can be difficult to gain access to this kind of data.

The closest option for finding these types of descriptions is Facebook ads, but the process will largely involve trial and error and testing over time. Is there an easier way or a different way to answer this question? Thankfully, the answer is yes. The following sections will examine various ways to find one's audience using a new way to define an audience: reader expectations.

Reader Groups

One way to ascertain reader expectations is to form a reader's group. A reader's group is a group, usually on Facebook, created by the author that is dedicated to readers of their books. Authors can ask questions to gain reader's interest, ask questions regarding upcoming or previous releases, and more. As the author receives feedback from their readers, he or she can determine what the readers are looking for in a book and plan accordingly. In addition to this, because the author is the administrator of the reader's group, they will have access to statistics which show various demographic information about the people who joined their group. This will also help to narrow down one's target readers.

Email List

Another option that is similar to creating a reader's group is to create an email list. Authors can market their email list in the front or back matter of their books, as well as through their websites and social media pages. With an email list, authors can ask questions and have direct conversations with readers in a more private setting. This may help the author to gain more in-depth information about what a reader is looking for in the genre the author writes in.

Author Pages

Another way to find readers is to create an author page. An author page can be created on Facebook, but Instagram, TikTok, and Twitter also allow options to sign up as an author and pose questions, excerpts, and more to gauge reader interests. If it seems there is a common response when it comes to a certain plot or subplot, genre or subgenre, or even character-type or trope, the author can use this information to plan their books.

Top 100 Lists

If an author doesn't enjoy using social media to find out what readers are looking for, there are other options. One of these options is to check the Top 100 list for the author's genre to see what kinds of titles, subtitles, and book descriptions are offered by the top selling books in the genre. Exploring this information and searching for commonalities can take out a lot of guesswork when trying to find one's audience.

Reviews Top 100 Books

Another way to gain access to information about what readers are looking for is to look at the reviews of the Top 100 author's books. Are there commonalities in what readers say they loved or hated about these books? Which types of characters did they like best? Which parts of the stories did they say they didn't care for? Readers can find all this information and more by looking at reviews. Authors can't accommodate all reader's expectations, but they can certainly target the most important ones.

Reviews on Your Books

In addition to looking at the reviews on the Top 100 author's books, authors can also look at reviews on their own books. Examine your own reviews the same way you would examine the Top 100 author's reviews. It is likely there will be similarities to what readers say about your books and the books of the authors who are selling well in your genre. Decide which factors are most important to focus on and make slight adjustments in your writing until you reach a point where things are running smoothly.

Release Strategies

There are numerous ways to launch a book, and no one strategy is superior to others. Some strategies only work sometimes, while others help to ensure success more frequently. The following sections will briefly discuss one method for releasing a series and one for releasing standalones.

Series

There are a few great ideas for releasing a series. One strategy is to release the first book but have at least the second book in the series on pre-order. This will help to increase sales for not only the first book but for subsequent books. Another option is to offer the first book in the series at a discounted price. In addition to this, linking the next book in the series to the end of all previous books helps to boost visibility and sales.

Standalones

When it comes to standalones, authors can build up excitement by either placing the book on pre-order and running ads, or sharing quotes, excerpts, cover reveals, and insights about the upcoming book during the time leading up to its release. Once it releases, authors can place book descriptions and links to other standalones at the end of the release. Directly linking to a similar standalone can help boost visibility and sales for both books.

Manuscript Optimization

I teach a course on book optimization where I cover much of what is discussed in previous sections of this book, along with additional information that will help authors produce manuscripts that put them in the best possible position for successful sales.

A few of the things I discuss in my course will be explained in the following sections. To learn more, email me to schedule a session at tanishastewart.author@gmail.com.

Author's Notes and Bios

Two elements that add a nice touch to a completed manuscript are author's notes and author bios. To distinguish between the two, an author's note is a brief (usually a page or less) letter to the reader at the beginning of a book (or the end, but I usually place it at the beginning), explaining the inspiration for the story or insights about the story that will help enhance the reader's experience. Author's notes provide a sense of connection between the reader and author because of their personal nature.

Author's notes can be structured in different ways, but I would suggest concluding the note with an invitation to leave a rating or review, join the author's email list, and connect with the author on social media. I suggest this as part of the author's note because it can help to form an instant connection with the reader before he or she begins the book.

I have had people sign up for my email list and reader's group by including these notes, and I have joined other author's email lists and reader's groups by doing the same. For an example of an author's note I wrote, check out [Should Have Thought Twice: A Psychological Thriller](#).

An author bio, like an author's note, can be structured in different ways, but the bio itself is a brief introduction to the author. Bios (usually included at the end of a book) provide a short description of the author's background, family, work outside of books, and book-related accomplishments. It can also include a fun or quirky fact about the author that will intrigue potential readers. For an example of an author bio, check mine out on my Amazon page.

Connecting Books

Another way to optimize one's manuscript is to provide the reader with the link to the author's next book after the last line of previous books. This is easy to do with series because all the author has to do is provide the link to the next book. With standalones, the process can work in multiple ways.

One suggestion is to link the book to another standalone that is in the same genre as the book the reader just finished. Another suggestion is to link the book to the first story in a series the author has written. The series should also be in the same or a similar genre as the book the author finished.

This small task can work wonders for an author's entire catalog. Readers can potentially go through all an author's books just by clicking the link to the next book at the end of the previous one.

Requesting Reviews

Another thing that will help to optimize one's manuscript is to request reviews. I previously mentioned requesting reviews in author's notes, but I also suggest authors request reviews after the last line of each of their manuscripts.

After linking the reader to another one of an author's books, authors should take the next line to request a rating or review of the book they just read. I like to include a brief instruction on what to mention in a review in case the reader feels like they don't know what to say. For an example of this, check out the final page of [Everybody Ain't Your Friend: An Urban Romance Thriller](#).

There are other things an author can do to optimize their books, but these three suggestions should help tremendously. To learn more about book optimization, take my course. Send me an email at tanishastewart.author@gmail.com to schedule a date.

Odds and Ends

The following section will discuss other things an author can do to enhance their credibility, boost visibility, and increase sales.

Cross-Promotions

Cross promotions can occur in multiple ways, but what it involves is teaming up with another author or group of authors who write in similar genres to promote one's books. Authors can collaborate by sharing each other's books to their email lists, reader's groups, author pages, and more. They can also participate in anthologies, where each author writes a story or chapter in a book or multi-volume works where each author writes a book in a series. Cross-promotions can be an effective tool to boost author's sales all around.

Review Swaps

Review swaps are exactly how they sound - an author selects a book from another author's catalog and leaves a review, and the other author does the same for them. This is a practice that is frowned upon and may lead to issues with KDP. The reason for this is that KDP considers these reviews to be unethical – the authors likely are providing five-star reviews for each other's books without even necessarily reading the book or offering an honest opinion. That being said, some authors participate in this practice to boost visibility and sales for their books.

Tagged Releases

Tagged releases occur when an author compiles a list of readers who agree to be tagged (on social media) in an author's upcoming release post when their book goes Live on Amazon. Tagged releases can be effective because they automatically boost visibility for the book to those who are tagged, as well as their followers. What helps even more is when people comment, react, and share the tagged post. Some authors have used this strategy to launch a #1 best-selling release.

Reader Engagement

Another strategy to boost visibility and sales is to join multiple reader's groups related to one's genre and engage with the readers in those groups. Comment on posts, respond to questions, and reply when someone engages with you. This will help generate organic relationships that can last the lifetime of an author's career.

Author Website

Building an author website that is interactive or provides space to subscribe to a mailing list can help boost sales and visibility dramatically. If the site is frequently updated with a blog and/or new releases, readers have a reason to keep visiting and purchasing an author's books. If the author uses a mailing list and offers a free incentive in the form of a bonus chapter or scene, bonus book, or other value-based material, it can increase reader engagement and retain the author's audience.

Amazon Author Central

Every published author should build their author central profile with at least an author photo and bio, and the site also allows to include other things like blogs, book trailers, and more. Having a professional looking Author Central account will boost an author's credibility and make readers more likely to buy their books.

Goodreads

One form of social media that is dedicated directly to books is Goodreads. Authors can join, add their books to the site, create profiles, host blogs and giveaways, recommend books, join reader's groups, and more. Once an author learns how this site works, it can be an effective tool for building a steady following of readers.

How to Publish on Kdp

This book contains a wealth of information regarding various aspects of writing, marketing, and publishing. One question that might remain is: how do I publish my book on kdp? This is a great question. The following will be a step-by-step guide.

First, the author needs to set up their account at kdp.com. This includes setting up payroll and tax information, so be sure to have this information handy.

Once the account is setup, the author is ready to publish their first book!

1. Go to the Bookshelf tab. There should be a button that says Create. Click it.
2. Next, the author will be led to a page with several options for creating eBooks, paperbacks, etc. Click Create eBook.
3. The first box on the next page asks an author to designate their language. For the purposes

of this tutorial, we will use the English language and assume the author is publishing in the United States. English is selected as the default language.
4. Next, type in the title and subtitle you plan to use for your book. Be sure to check for spelling and capitalization in the title because this cannot be changed once the book is published. For the subtitle, KDP allows authors to change their subtitles on eBooks but not paperbacks or hardcovers. Please bear this in mind when choosing a subtitle. Also note that the main title must match the title provided on the cover of the book or KDP will reject it.
5. After this, there is an option to add series information if this book is part of a series. If this book is not part of a series, you can skip to the next part. If this book is not part of a series now but becomes part of a series later, you can always update this information through the Bookshelf tab.
6. Next, KDP asks for the edition number. If this is the first edition of the book, leave it blank.
7. The next field contains space for the author to provide their name. Provide the pen name you wish to use for this book. Please note that the pen name an author uses has to match the author's name on the cover of the book or it will be rejected.

8. After this, there are options to add other contributors. I always add my pen name again as an author. The reason for this is that if an author does not add their pen name in this area, sometimes their name won't show up on the book's Amazon page, but the other contributor's names will. This happened with my debut novel, Even Me, and I had to go back and add my name to this section in order for it to show up. The next person to add is your editor, if you wish for their name to be linked to your book on Amazon, as well as your cover designer (title would be illustrator). To add editors and illustrators, click the button that says Add Another.
9. Now comes the fun part: entering your book description. I usually try to prepare mine before I log into KDP to upload my books, but in general, keep the book description short and punchy with words and imagery that will entice the reader to buy the book.
10. After this, you will need to indicate your publishing rights. If you are the originator of the book, click the first option.
11. Now it's time to enter keywords. Generate genre-specific terms that will help place your book in front of the right readers. The more specific your terminology, the better (i.e., African American suspense thriller versus suspense thriller). Be sure to use all seven spaces provided.

12. Next, it's time to enter the categories for your book. Choose the best two options available that pertain to your book and its genre (to learn more about categories, sign up for my Book Optimization course).
13. The next section asks for the age and grade range. Leave this blank, unless you are writing a children's book or erotica.
14. After this, you will need to decide when you are publishing your book. If you are ready to publish now, choose the first option. Note: If you choose the option to set up your book for pre-order, your final manuscript has to be submitted by a certain date and time or you will lose all presales of your books and possibly be penalized by not being able to place another book on pre-order for a year. KDP allows up to two extensions per year on pre-ordered books, but once these options are exhausted, the author loses the right to place a book on pre-order for a year. This can also cause the author's credibility to decrease in reader's eyes.
15. Click save and continue to be brought to the next screen.
16. The next part asks for your preferences for Digital Rights Management. I always choose Enable DRM because it helps to safeguard your book against pirates.
17. After this, choose whether your book is ready to upload now (ready to publish) or if it is on

pre-order, you can choose to upload the finished version closer to the due date.
18. Next is the cover. You can create one via Kindle Creator, but I would highly suggest hiring a cover designer or creating your own cover via another platform like Canva, GIMP, or Photoshop.
19. After this, you have the option to preview how your book will look on a Kindle device. I always scroll through the pages to ensure everything lines up properly. If it doesn't, you can upload a new version of the book and preview that until everything looks how you want it to.
20. The next section asks for ISBN information. This is unnecessary for eBooks.
21. Click save and continue to be brought to the next screen.
22. The next section asks whether you want to enroll your book in KDP Select (KU). I always choose this option because it helps yield the most sales, especially for a new author.
23. The next part asks where your book will be sold. I always keep the first option selected for worldwide territories.
24. Next, the author must choose their primary marketplace. If in the United States, choose Amazon.com (the default option).
25. After this, choose the royalty percentage you wish to earn and set the price. Be sure to

study the Top 100 list in your genre to ensure that you are using a comparable price.
26. Once you have done this, scroll down to submit your book. Congratulations! After the eBook is submitted, similar guidelines can be followed for paperbacks and hardcovers. Please note that eBooks are typically available for sale within a couple of hours, but they can take up to 72 hours (or longer) based on KDP's schedule. Paperbacks and Hardcovers typically take 24 hours, but can also take longer due to KDP's schedule.

If you prefer to have someone walk you through the process, email me at tanishastewart.author@gmail.com and we can schedule an appointment to publish your book!

About the Author

Tanisha Stewart was born and raised in Springfield, Massachusetts. She graduated with a Bachelor of Science in Psychology and Sociology in 2009, as well as a Master of Psychology in 2011. She is a college professor, teaching psychology (which she loves). In addition to her career as a lecturer, Tanisha has been writing for as long as she can remember, creating realistic story lines, relatable characters, and multi-layered plots that almost everyone can enjoy. She also takes part in hobbies such as performing rap and spoken word for various audiences.

Tanisha not only demonstrates a passion for writing through her vivid story lines; she is also committed to helping other writers succeed. She offers author coaching, editing, formatting, and ghostwriting services to help aspiring authors get their work off the ground, and to see it through to completion. In additional to this, she hosts Book Optimization and Amazon Ads courses. You can find out more about Tanisha and these services at www.tanishastewartauthor.com.

If you would like to connect with Tanisha Stewart via social media, here are her contacts (she would love to hear from you!):

Website: www.tanishastewartauthor.com
Facebook: Tanisha Stewart, Author
Reader's Group (Facebook): Tanisha Stewart Readers
Twitter: TStewart_Author
Instagram: tanishastewart_author
TikTok: @authortanishastewart
Gmail: tanishastewart.author@gmail.com
Amazon: Tanisha Stewart (follow me!)
YouTube: Tanisha Stewart (subscribe!)

www.ingramcontent.com/pod-product-compliance
Lightning Source LLC
Chambersburg PA
CBHW071418210526
45465CB00001B/440